HOW IT FEELS?

A BOOK ON RELATIVITY OF THOUGHTS

GURPREET KASHAB

ISBN 979-888569794-1

Contents

Foreword

In 2017,when I was about to enjoy the peak of my self confidence,suddenly everything shattered as my expectations were not met by the results from my efforts.Very soon I began recompiling my lost inner self confidence and made it worth it by proving myself.But in the next moment,due to some unavoidable repercussions of anxiety episodes,i lost it all again.But I never stopped myself from putting efforts even during the hopeless days.I saw it,i grew through it and I learnt through it.Whatever I learnt from that very phase,i thought to write it all to help other going through the same phase.Hopefully I am growing through even now.Wishing readers a healing experience as they read this book.

Thank You.

I

You Don't Know, How It Feels??

You don't know, what it feels !!

I am the one

Who you consider none, I live among you all

But I struggle to search my soul I see myself doing alone

Even in the crowd, but when I discover something new

I feel proud.

Unlike you, I see myself overdo, Even when there is no anxiety ,

You do hang out in public,But I see nobody for me in society

I want to tabulate Don't rather dissociate

You make fun of my depression, feels like suppression

I feel abandoned

I want to conclave

But nobody is my friend

As I am a despondent slave.

.

You may not fraternise what I feel,,

Life is uncertain yet challenging....

Life is so uncertain yet challenging, But to accept this challenge,

I have no zeal

You might not know what it feels, You might not know, what it feels...

But on the contrary side

Life is fascinating, full of delight The ecstasy is angelic

All knowing has made it all.

He filled the essence of compassion,

In creature's soul

The struggles you see, The hassles you see,

To be what you yearn for It is all god's plan,

There is lot to explore

Life is a rollercoaster yet graceful fair But never be cynistic

Don't you dare

Fill it with heart and grace

So life can be a beautiful race..

II

Melancholy

Often they say, melancholy is the happiness of being sad. Ever heard about this word? "Melancholy "Our answer to such words usually what does that mean?. Perhaps Melancholy is a situation of pensive sadness and a feeling of depression. The importance of mental health is usually ignored. But with increasing stress in our lifestyle we find us to be falling into a deep pit Of sadistic and upsetting thoughts Which often disturbs the peace of mind.

It is now important for us all to normalise and emphasise on the importance of mental health and understand the state of mind of a person

undergoing it.

Many a times, we misinterpret & misunderstand the two wide terms depression and fatigue. In reality these two terms have far different definitions but are often related. A person suffering from depression may or may notexperience fatigue. Similarly a person said experiencing fatigue may not be actually depressed .This is similar to what we say two sides of the same coin.

Fatigue can be linked to depression but we should not consider a person is depressed , If he or she is tired from his or her work. Also it is true that a depressed person can feel fatigue or tiredness due
to his or her lack of interest in activities. However, not everytime depression or mental challenges make you feel tired.
Being Depressed or having a belief of disquietness is often seen many a times in human life. It is absolutely normal to feel low

when you are actually heedless about the reason of brawl in the mind. In fact, it is scientifically proven that serotonin –a hormone , Controls the extent of happiness and sadness of human being. It is absolutely normal when there is rise and fall in its levels. However, diagnosing the elevations and downfall of this Happy neurotransmitter, at right time is essential.

But what is the basic need of understanding the importance of one's mental well-being? Simple answer to this important yet modest question is that one must understand all shades of human nature. Human behaviour is a very wide and interesting topic that needs to be understood and studied. Every aspect of human behaviour is based on various complex beliefs which makes up a beautiful human life.

Talking about ups and downs in a person's life, we must emphasise on the struggles of a person. Respecting one's struggle, out of what he or she has made his or her life, is important. Struggles make a human being wise and shapes him into perfectionist. Whatever a person achieves in his or her life is all because of the struggles. It is important to keep the mindset strong during

such times. Keeping a positive mindset and a goal with continuous deletion of negative thoughts is important for one to achieve satisfaction in human life. It is all about the mindset of an individual. But it is not easy to stay calm and have a positive outlook all the time. After all it is a human nature. But the thing that matters is to have a calm and supportive response in situation that tends to disturb the peace of mind. Being healthy also attributes to the health of mind. Since it is human nature to feel low sometimes,but in some this feeling converts into
sadness.

This Enlarges to such an extent that a person loses his interest in vital activities. There is a pensive sadness which might be due to a specific reason and sometime without any reason. .A t such times when a person's mental state gets disturbed, the person incorporates a feeling of loneliness and finds no one around him for emotional support. This is sometimes not observed by people around such person because he limits his social presence by limiting the extent of conversation to people around him. He becomes socially awkward.

But for others it might not be evident because of developing self centric nature of the modern human race. The situation of the sufferer, by then, is diagnosed as disturbed mental health balance. The behaviour of such person may very from person-to-person. Some don't let it affect their professional lives while some find themselves lost in life.Disturbed mental peace often causes the sense of brawl in mind which some way or the other affects the thought process of a person. The important thing is the realistaion of the fact that mental health is deteriorating day by day.

III

How does a person feel?

An individual suffering from a mental disturbance has a lot of things going on in his mind. To feel the extent of brawl is the most difficult thing for a normal person but it is even more difficult for the sufferer to live in such situation.

One who goes through such phase often find himself surrounded by a bunch of negative thoughts. He finds himself in a deep pit like situation from where he wants to escape but he could not. He feels alone even in public. He

limits his social life and isolates himself .He finds himself stuck in various situations. There occur plenty of instances which makes him challenge his strengths. He finds himself surrounded by double mindedness. Such a person often becomes an over thinker for most of times. He becomes unproductive in his work field because of the useless Brawl in his head. There is no sign of hope fullness or hope that can make him overcome

the mental depression. A sense of insecurity prevails in his mind. There is a feeling of sadness, grief, hopelessness, and insecurity building a home inside such a person. These all qualities lead to the formation of another quality such as building of anger, impatience, jealousy and most importantly a sense of under confidence.

The worst part of a person who goes through such heavy phase of life is ,The fact that, this part of life breaks the self- confidence of a person due to constant failures. One tries to keep some positivity in his mind to keep himself going on the harsh part of life, but the duration of positivity in such phase is very little. Most of

the time this positivity is put down by rising levels of negative thoughts, self doubt, in securities and most importantly by the past instances that lead a person to such phase which constantly reminds him to stop due to fear of failure.

Self-doubt is another aspect of this phase. The constant fear of uncertain insecurity tries hard to limit the capabilities of such person there is always a feeling of self doubt that limits the strengths of that person and this feeling give rise to quite a bunch of negative thoughts. But, what all are these "negative thoughts "?

often we hear about the fact that negative thought should be completely eradicated so as to live a peaceful life full of satisfaction. These negative thoughts are nothing but the reason behind the person who gives up easily without trying to achieve success due to fear of failure. Also, there is a fear about what if "society "considers them a failure. The self-doubt

extends to such an extent that a fear of being present in social gatherings also develops. Such a person tries to avoid the interaction and develops a sense of insecurity that makes him feel awkward to share his state of mind. There is a feeling that a person standing next to him must be Thinking about him and that thought would certainly be a negative quality about him. Such a feeling is what we call insecurity. Having such a feeling and it self is quite dangerous because it directly influences the state of mind.

All in all these qualities directly or indirectly disturbs the balanced state of mind and develops an altered mindset that tries to do everything differently. There is far different approach to every single thing. A different lifestyle, begins the path of a life, which is very different from normal life but the only thing that is same is the physical presence of a person in both the worlds – normal life and introvert life. Another major habit seen in a person's behavior during such chapter is mood swings. Mood Can be defined as a state of mind and swings here refers to the fluctuation in the state. Apparently there is an inconsistency in such persons social graces repeatedly.

Sometimes a happy state of mind changes to sheer sadness in a jiffy. A person becomes unpredictable in severe cases. But on the thoroughgoing, and observer can clearly observe the symptoms of a disturbed psychological state of such individual.

In most of theCases the common sign of low spirits involves lack of interest or may even include continuous feeling of dysphoria or sadness. In other cases lack of sleep or even oversleeping syndrome maybe present. All in all the symptoms of such ailment can vary from person to person depending on the kinds And the reason behind the fact that caused such a condition.

Not only depression, but such state of mind can cause other major issues.

IV

What struggles one face?

Struggle is one of the most important word in the book called life. If a dictionary is smelled out to quest the meaning Of this prominent word, struggle can be elucidated as a fight In which somebody tries to do or achieve something which is near to impossible.

When a person makes a tremendous amount of effort to make all the things right that paves the way to his ultimate goal., The difficulties that he faces and the way he deals and overcomes them all, is known as struggle.

Struggle is when you see the rise in the obstructions that hardens your way to get Your goal. Struggle is the phase which makes or breaks the soul or spirit of a person. it is the time period that every human being goes through sooner or later in his life. It is always said widely that a person goes through four stages of life namely childhood adolescence period, adulthood and the old age. But never do they say that if you have to progress through these stages in life, you have to overcome some hurdles too.

Importantly, these hurdles are essentialto make us experience the essence of various emotions. The feeling of satisfaction, the wrath of jealousy, the essence of kindness, the warmth of happiness, the wrath of anger, essence of

individuality, the pain of passion, The urge of achieving, the satisfaction after victory, are all because of these so called hurdles. This emotions are brought out of the human soul by a process that must be and is usually considered essential.This is nothing but struggle.

Struggle makes you experience all these emotions. Struggle makes you feel low sometimes but at the end, you achieve success not only because you thought of a goal but because of the hard work that you did to achieve your goal. The hardships that you go through and the way you handle your ups and downs, makes no one except you, a better, stronger, wiser and true human being.

The kind of attitude or mindset that you build In your inner self is very important not only when one feels demotivated or demoralized but also when you have achieve the goal. The hardships that you face, the failures that you go through are

only because of some reason. Feel yourself fortunate to struggle, to have gotten the

problems to deal with because that is the only way one Can feel grateful and satisfied to an extent when we grow through. Although no human stay fully satisfied due to the urge to achieve more. due to which, there is something you find missing in that to do check list waiting to be checked.

In practical life, this thought is important to be had. After all, every man is the architect of his destiny. The fact is that how this destiny is shaped for brighter and better things to go through depends only upon the extent of hard work and the passionyou have to achieve the ultimate intent.

It is an age old saying that:

> ***"there is scarcely any passion without struggle"***

Jazmin

- Albert Camus.

The point of discussion here encourages the need to work harder and harder. This hard work is nothing but the way that leads you to your goal. The kind of difficulties, failures, bullying, insensitivity that you face during this road of life is what we say struggle. Another important lesson that life teaches every human being on his way of hard work and struggle is the importance of patience. As they say, great things take time but the question is how long is this time?. We must have seen many around us getting success in a short span of time while many of us have to wait for a much longer duration.

Sometimes one gets an easy success regarding which he feels immense happiness for a fraction of moments but sooner or later that achievement tends to be worthless and is taken for granted. This is the reason why such people, who get easy success, are more vulnerable to be affected deeply and hence causing disturbance in the state of mind.Easy achievement

accordingly may benefit one for few moments but for long run, it becomes difficult as such a person might have never seen any failure thereforeeven a single wrongdoing or failure might hit him hard. The situation becomes extremely dangerous when the question arises on one's self- confidence. On the other hand, when a person who finds it so much difficult on his Way to success, when Achieves it after a very huge amount of struggle, he celebrates his victory in much more sophisticated and mature manner.

The essence of patience, hard work and compassion in his heart makes him feel even more special, even on his smaller achievements.This is the reason why hard earned success is said to be of much more worth than easy getter. The period struggle is basically as important as essential needs for human survival because it builds the key element of human survival that is resistance. Resistance here can be referred to a state of mind which can adapt itself in any situation and act accordingly.

The persuasion of struggle that one undergoes can be different for different individuals. A person usually takes in sometime to understand and perceive through what exactly is going on in his life. This span of time can vary accordingly. Usually, we see, Two kinds of people, on broad classification-ones being extroverts and other being introverts

What exactly is meant by such terms and what different struggles do they face?

Usually we come around people who are somewhat open mindedand express themselves openly without fearing about what others will think. Such kind of people are often happy at any situation of life and try to maintain positivity even in the toughest situation.

Such are what we call extroverts. On the other side, there are people who feel comfortable only with limited number of people around them.

Nature of such persons is usually shy. They fear while interacting. By the way, such people usually don't interact much with strangers. They don't express openly. They try to settle the brawl of their head within themselves. Such are introverts.

While a normal person is usually referred by what we say extrovert, an introvert person, in my opinion, has two sides of his personality. The foremost part of his personality is what He is when he is alone.

Alone in the sense that the quality of thoughts that he or she keeps in mind but don't usually express them. This kind of personality is fluctuating within itself. There are times when one is in happy mood and is open for conversations with one who he is comfortable with.The another part is when he is in the public or in social gathering. He finds himself stuck in dilemma whether he wants to speak up something due to which he keeps his thoughts in his head and prepares a speech in his own head but finds it difficult to gather courage to express himself.He feels socially awkward by thinking upon the opinions of others which does not exist in real. The struggle in being underconfident and then all the stressful opinions of other bother him so much. On the other hand extroverts to face such struggles. But the reason why they don't carry any baggage in their head. This baggages of stress.

They do feel stressed just like others, after all, they too are human beings. But the fact is that they remove it all from their head by expressing themselves to others or paying attention to some other issues which are of No such importance, just to remove stress. Also they hang out with like-minded people but on the opposite side introverts just get in entangled within themselves. Introverts easily get stressed out and due to which they constantly find themselves to be in continuous chain of negative thoughts.

All in all, it is all about the perception. It is about how you handle the situation. The struggles are essential, that is what makes up human mind strong. The struggle phase lets us analyse the extent of pain that one can bear. The struggle that one faces on his own path of achieving success, to fulfil his goal can be uncertain. This goal is not certainly about career aspect. Different people have different aspirations. The definition of success is also different for every individual. Some find success when they achieve their career related goals, some feel happy to be peaceful, some stay happy in what they have while some always complain for what they don't have.

For some success is the peace in their personal lives, for some Success is being loved by the chosen one and for some success is when they fulfil Their desire of materialistic Things. Many of us, judge the success of a person by his or her financial status or how powerful his or her position is. These all judgements are an overview of definition, what society sets.

These judgements make barriers for a normal person who wants to do something extraordinary apart from just being normal. On collecting experiences of life and Carefully observing The necessity of life, it can be

confidently said that, the highest amount of wealth or fortune that one earned during his life is nothing as compared to the one who is satisfied and peaceful at mind. The difficulties on the path of peace are greater in mind than in real .But the passion to keep overcoming struggles in life, the enthusiasm to keep moving, the stubborn nature of achieving something, these are what it takes to peaceful and satisfied life.

Struggle is natural. Even nature selects the best among us. But becoming the best itself is a struggle. All in all struggle brings out our best version.

V

Mood Swings

Often we hear many people complaining about mood swings. They either try to blame, All their mistakes of behaviour, on mood swings or they tend to cover up using such term. What actually are those mood swings? Actually it is a non-scientific term which literally means sudden change in behaviour pattern of person. As the name suggests, mood swings simply define any kind of fluctuation in behaviour of a person. As the swing moves forward and backward in the shape of curve, similarly the mood or behaviour of a person too seems to fluctuate.This oscillation in the frame of mind can occur due to many reasons.

We often misinterpret the word "mood swings"and often relate it to women,most of the times. This means that we often think that only women undergo mood swings due to a natural process. But this is half truth. Mood fluctuation can occur to any human regardless of gender.The important fact that needs to be checked while we think of this, is that it is absolutely normal to show abrupt changes in behaviour. It is natural. After all, it is a part of human nature.

There is nothing wrong in being emotional sometimes. Being human, it is okay to express the way you feel. Sometimes people are afraid to show their natural feelings, as a result of which their feelings of anger keeps on piling up in their own mind. This, in fact, is very harmful for the balance of mind. The constant suppression of feelings Like pain, agony, misery, despondency, sadness and other bitter sweet feelings keep on building an empire in the mind of such person.

But there comes a time, when the person is unable to cumulate any more feeling, he finds

himself helpless and finds no way other than break down. In such cases people who keep their emotions intact, tend to break down at some point or the other.

On the contrary side, some people do not hesitate to bring out whatever they feel. Such people don't care over the judgement passed by society. This is how a person should be. The essence of being genuine about the tangibility is fascinating to observe.It is even more beautiful when you realise that it has become natural instinct of your soul. To become emotionless, as some say, is greatest mistake that a human could make according to me. The fact is that, to be emotional is just equivalent to be normal. Let's just not judge anyone on the basis of how they feel. Everybody has a right to express themselves.

Sometimes, due to some particular situation a person may not find it a way to burst out his feelings. But remember, there is nobodyWho has never cried. It is fine to cry out.

It is absolutely fine to say what you feel. Coming back to the topic of the talk, mood swings, it is important for us to differentiate mood swings from the situational mood or behaviour.

In simple words, there maybe fluctuation in your mood depending upon the situations you face. There can be a time when you may feel a sense of happiness but if you come across a bad news, it is natural that you would feel sorry for the bad news.

Eventually, there can be the reasons for why you change your behaviour. But on the other side the fluctuation in behaviour is without any particular reason and the behaviour shows a feeling of happiness at the moment and feeling of pensive sadness at another, this can be considered as a case of mood swings. This is because the reason of this change does not exist. if we ask a person encountering mood swings on regular basis, about the reason behind their mood swings, the person may not be able to elaborate. He or she might say that "I felt that ". Every particular feeling has its own essence and normally is expressed because of a reason. But in a depressed state of mind or an unbalanced

state of mind, a person might express his feelings without any reason. The sheer transformation of Propensity is often seen in such cases.

If we study mood swings on a wider scale., We might know the reasons behind them. Sometimes one can go through it due to change in the sleep wake cycle of a person. It is scientifically proven that a sleep of at least 6 to 8 hours is necessary for a human body to function properly .this is important because it is the process that helps in restoring various vital systems and it plays an essential role in checking the balance of various hormones in the body. Lack of sleep may cause hormonal imbalance which accounts for another reason for more fluctuations.

Other reasons may include mental disorders like bipolar, clinical depression and also the disorders related to central nervous system. Mood swings are generally common in

pregnancy phase in women. genetic reasons may also be credited in some cases. Mood swings are not situational but a repercussion of feelings. This may sound a bit illogical but sometimes a situation can be as normal as it can be, however one might have various feelings based on perception.

It is absolutely normal, as we said earlier, to show what you feel. But sometimes the mood fluctuations can cause the trauma when things get normal. A person undergoing all this could even get a feeling of getting uncontrollable at times.

To get a control of one's own individuality, one must have a control or learn to manage his or her mood.

This can be achieved by two way. The first way out is to follow the law of natureand not disturbing the chain of continuity. In simple words, one should take proper amount of sleep along with various physical exercise so as to keep his or her hormones in balance.Another way to reach this balance is by receiving help

from others by undergoing behaviour therapies that can manage your emotions.

All in all there is nothing to be ashamed of. It is human nature to be a showpiece of emotions. But also remember that overdoing anything is harmful. The thing that matters is the balance and balancing emotions sometimes becomes crucial.

Always remember that you are going to be known by the product of your struggles. Expressing right emotions at appropriate places without any pressure is how it should go.

Never express a feeling when it is forced by someone. Express it only when you feel it.

> ***Do it, not to please anyone but to satisfy your own soul. Nevertheless, it is rightly said to go with what your heart says. So be true to yourself and you can live***

peacefully.

VI

Importance of having a goal

Many beautiful sayings often come from great personalities. The "Great "personalities were not great by birth. they were great because of their great experiences, efforts and mindset. One such great philanthropist and activist was an American professional boxer, Muhammad Ali.The greatest message he ever conveyed was the message that had the power to empower or motivate someone. In few words, he conveyed the reason behind every successful person on the earth. He said :

– what keeps me going is goals.

Jazmin

These few words if understood deeply, can even change the perception of an individual. For some these maybe regular words, some might ignore it as useless grammatically incorrect line. But these words are a story in their own. In real life, we see all of us running around.We all put our efforts and energy to achieve success.

But, what success really means? Why do we run behind everything possible to achieve success?

The answers to these questions is simple yet complicated. This might sound weird because anything without any complication is said to be simple. Then, why is the answer simple yet complicated?

It is simple because saying anything is easy but when it comes to achieving,the path is complicated.Yet it is really important to have a goal because perseverance is the key. Different people have different mindsets. It is the mindset that makes or breaks a person. You might not have enough resources to fulfil what your heart says but one thing, like good intentional mindset, can be the reason for your success. It is rightly said that :

> *without dreams and goals there is no living, only merely existing, and is not why we are here.*
>
> *-Mark Twain*

Jazmin

Mark Twain, expressed his wonderful thoughts in these words.

To have a goal is like being driver of a car. This car has to reach a destination. The destination is what we say, success.Many a times, this car needs maintenance. This maintenance can be related to the reality checks that you face in the form of struggle and failure. The road on which the car is meant to be driven is what we call life.the car in fact, can be thought of individuality. All in all it is the destination or the goal which can be achieved only if all goes well. This is how life goes. You set up some goals with either materialistic intention or for spiritual satisfaction. Having either of them is absolutely fine.

For all the achievements to be achieved, There must have been some goal or motive behind it. In simple words, to achieve something you should have a reason to do so. For example, if you are studying hard for attaining a degree,you must have a reason that why are you doing so. Continuing with that example, the goal must have been to achieve a career-based success after doing a degree.

The life which we are living should always have a reason to live. For that, it is important that you have some goals to achieve. To fulfil your dreams, you must have a logical dream first. After that you must realise the importance of turning that dream into reality. This is where we are required to plan the way through which we can accomplish and bring our dream to a successful conclusion. This is where we need to set goals.

Goals can be divided into many types.

Sometimes we set up large goals in our mind. A large goal is simply the thing that requires a lot of effort and time to be achieved. For that purpose we need to take small steps. To reach the terrace you have to take stairs usually. Similarly to achieve a big goal,It is sum total of the small achievements that will take us further. Many a times we hear of short- term goals. Basically short-term goals are the ones which are easily achievable but that too requires a lot of hard work and concentration and sincerity as well.

The short-term goals are Usually set up for accomplishing in near future. Time and again, if we put up a constant effort to achieve something really big, short-term goals help us do so. The importance of having an aim in life is that we can avoid negative thoughts by doing so. If we keep ourselves busy then there is nothing like overthinking in our head. We can divert our mind from depressive thinking by keeping our focus on our aim.Often we say " I am doing everything possible to achieve my goal but things are not going as per my plan and …….”.

In such case, the realisation of the fact that something is wrong, in processing ,is necessary. There may be a slight lack of effort or there must be a slight reduction in concentration. In fact, the art of being focused is difficult to practise in modern times. With increasing methods of technology and media, the amount of distraction is also increasing. There is a lesser time left for concentration.Most of the distraction occurs from the social media. In this era of social media, more and more people are coming up and are actively using social media.

Being a user of social media is not a bad thing but overdoing anything is harmful as said earlier many times. However, there are some benefits of social media like interaction and being aware of the things happening around us and worldwide. But on the other hand we tend to forget that over using and spending more and more hours on it can misbalance our plan for achieving Desired goal. Keeping ourselves away from the distraction requires a strong mindset. This can be acquired when it comes from within us.

The only motivation that can keep you going is the one that you give to yourself. Thus, it is important to realise, understand and work upon the need, processing and attaining a good result from our efforts.

Goals are magical. They have the power to change the entire motive of existence of an individual. The purpose of existing is the fact that an individual aspires to have a dream and accomplish it bydoing every possible effort. The happiness and satisfaction will be worthit. After all your effort you will realise that how important was it for your growth and mental health. All your despondencies, The failures you faced, they all made you realise the importance of every little achievement that you had made.

To have a goal and to struggle simultaneously to achieve that goal, is What that forms the basis of life. Life is nothing but the collection of memories-good or bad, struggles, failures and all your achievements.

Enjoy the every moment that you live to feel the gratitude of being in existence. Life is wonderful but only when you see it's positive

side.

VII

How to find a motivation?

Human life is all about the experiences that you earn. it is the power of a soul that searches for peace throughout its life span.There may be some who achieve their goal in single attempt while some face failure as already discussed.

The thing that is important as a result of such situation is perception. How do you perceive such achievements or failures? It all depends on how we want to see it. For example, if you achieve your desiredaim at once then you get a responsibility of maintaining the efforts involved in doing so. The responsibility is given to you by your own brain.The other outlook to this success is when you don't appreciate the importance of your achievement and take it for

granted.

This can further develop a sense of overconfidence in mind. It creates a false narrative about how easy it was for you to do this thing. This is when you don't realise its worth. Sooner or later you when you get your first failure, it might Affect you so badly to a greater extent. Apart from this, there are people who see multiple failures even before taking the first step towards their goals .this is often Seen when a person is underconfident about the potential that he has within himself. Failures do not certainly define the extent of the lack in your effort. Instead, the ability to accept and work upon your failures is the thing that gets you a bigger success.

For most of us, failures bring along a sense of insecurity and sadness. It is the time when there is complete lack of motivation. In fact, we are unable to find a reason that whether we should continue on the path to pursue that dream.But, failures are what the universe sends us to realise our inner potential and bring out The best in us.

Universe is nothing but everything. Some find the universe in the name of religion. But universe lies within us. Human soul is the only soul that has ability to do wonders.Universe is

everywhere. Human soul is the universe.

Now talking about the lack of motivation when we go through a certain failure, we must first realise its importance. Motivation, according to grammar, means the formation of a reason that guides you to the right direction.Motivation is anything that keeps your spirits high. It is the chain of thoughts that have The power to enlighten one's mind and give him a reason to continue on the way to achieve his goal. Motivation is the hardest thing to find in today's world.

With increasing stress, lifestyle of the human race to tends to mutate. Each one of us is running to achieve. Each one of us feel stress while overthinking About the negative consequences. This has led to the creation of a sluggish lifestyle which does not involve the physical or mental growth or satisfaction.

It has now become the reason for most of us facing difficulty in socialising and expressing our thoughts to anyone around us.We feel shy to talk about the fact thatwe want help due to the

fear of embarrassment. It is the reason behind the fact that finding motivation has now become a difficult task to do.Contrary to this fact, it is true that for a person who has undergone self-realisation, finding motivation is no big deal.

For such a person,Everything around him is a motivation. From his daily experiences he may realise something good or bad about the others. He, too can feel the sadness that comes along with his low times but he quickly can overcome his sadness or feeling of insecurity by realising that What he exactly needs at that point of time. To lighten his mood or state of mind, he can do anything that makes him happy. Soon he realises the need of motivation and can find it from his experiences. A person can be motivated in two ways mainly. These ways to get the motivation depends upon the source , that is, from where is that origination of motivation coming from.The first way to get a motivation is from an external source.This external source can be any other person who has the potential to encourage you

with the powers of his words. The motivation that he imbibes in you, increases your morals and lets you feel enthusiastic. The power of motivating another person is very unique to

find.Other external sources can be watching someone who gives you motivation or taking help from someone who you find an inspiration.

But there are times when we don't Have anyone around us. For most of the times we are with our own self rather than people around us. At such time, when there is a need of motivation, one finds it difficult to search for a motivator it is the time that makes us realise something really important. It is the time during which one needs self motivation. Self motivation can be included in internal source of motivation. Internal source of motivation refers to the motivation that comes from our inner self. It is of the utmost importance that we realise the fact that one needs his own self to keep him going. Motivating ourselves by our own thoughts is the thing that helps us for long run. Often we see people getting highly enthusiastic after somebody else's motivational Session. But this enthusiasm is short lived and motivational thoughts are usually overcome by negative and anxious thoughts. Due to this we keep seeking for motivation. On the other hand, when we find the motivation from our own thoughts we can primarily achieve two things at the same time.

One, that is obvious, is that we can keep ourselves motivated and other is the fact that we can actually overcome the process of

overthinking, nervousness, self-doubt, negative thoughts and sadness now the question arises that how do we motivate ourselves?

This is another great question to be answered.We can motivate ourselves in several ways. The first and the foremost way is to appreciate and feel happy for even the smallest achievements that you achieve. This is highly beneficial as it builds the self-confidence and helps in removing self-doubt and fear of achieving milestones. Surround yourself with positivity and the things that keeps you happy. It is very difficult but once it is perceived to be good it becomes easy.After all it is all about the way in which we see the situation in.

Always be optimistic And leave a scope of correction within you. Always think of happiness as the thought of being happy leads to increased level of happy hormone that keeps you strong mentally .If you are mentally strong, you can achieve physical strength because you have that potential of achieving so due to a strong mindset.Always think of positivity and try to lessen or reduce the negativity. Maintain a distance from those affecting your mental

equilibrium. that is how we can keep our lives going. That is how we can learn to live.

VIII

The essence of being an individual

Have you ever thought of the fact that in the whole world, among population of billions, you have some unique characteristic features that accounts for your individuality. The life, that you are living, only belongs to you. There is nobody else that can ever take your place. This is because you exist and occupy the place that defines your life in existence. This means that you are important in whatever way it has to be. This means that you are special. This all has been said and heard enough times to make us all aware, realise and understand the concept of individuality.

Individuality, means a sense of being aware of one's own importance in life and realising the fact that human being is the strong enough even when one is alone. It does not necessarily means that one must stay alone or isolated to realise his or her individuality. Rather it is the process of appreciating and getting an idea of self-worth and also understanding the calibre that a person carries in himself. Individuality refers to a feeling that makes a person realise the set of priorities that one has to put ahead of every single causative agent that intends to disturb his mindset.

The basic characteristic of every successful person in this world is individuality. Successful people are recognised from far away because they carry themselves as a complete package like a team. But wait, success is not measured by the amount of wealth or fortune one makes or the number of cars or luxuries one owns. Success is when you are able to fulfil even little dream or goal of yours. Success is when you are satisfied in the duty that you perform.Satisfaction is another trait of an individual who can discover his own self.

Coming back to importance of individuality, it is one of the greatest concerns that one must realise the individuality comes from every little effort that one makes to achieve his or her desires. It comes when you know that you have the potential of doing things which others refrain themselves from doing so. Individuality is all about the set of decisions that you make that gives the positive results for you. It is the discovery of a persons self trust. Individuality is something that builds self-confidence in a person. It makes a person assured of certain things because such a person is confident about those things because of self belief.

When a person is aware of the individuality that he or she carries, there is nothing that can stop him or her from going onto the path that leads him or her to a life full of satisfaction.

The depressing thoughts, that are very common in today's lifestyle, have a potential to disturb and obstruct a person of even a strong individuality. But with a positive mindset and a feeling of hope fullness and optimism, one can overcome such phase by keeping himself aware

about his self-worth. It is of no surprise that even a person who had realised the importance of his individuality can also go through phase of anxiety, stress and depression. After all, the feeling of sadness is normal. But as already said, excess of everything has its own harms. But such an individual can overcome such phase in a shorter duration of time because he or she is aware that It is only the self confidence that matters the most. Individuality is helpful most of the times. The only purpose of life, for some people who are oriented more towards the thought processes, is realising and finding the reason for one's existence. Life is all about experiences and these experiences always teach us the various aspects of life. These aspects of life are only learnt when you learn the positive effects of that particular experience which is only possible when you have the ability to think deeply and analyse.

This is possible only when you are willing to accept and understand the changes around you. These all make a person empower his or her individuality as he or she is now aware of the pattern of lessons that life teaches.

Apart from all this, individuality is the power that one has, to differentiate among the rights and wrongs. It accounts for the decisions that you make and tips you give to upcoming generations. Individuality is a moral approach. It is a right to have something Unique in your presence that makes you a person to be remembered. Individuality is what makes you special.

Being a person of different set of thoughts thatare right according toone's own self, is what it takes to make one different from others.

Individuality is an art. Individuality paints your personality. It improves and enhance your moral existence. It keeps yourself enlightened. It builds a confidence inside yourself to stand by your point of view. It gives Strength to your feelings and hence people find you stronger mentally.

As an individual, a person is aware of his or her goals and aims along with need or reason to achieve that goal. Such person is well aware of his or her responsibilities in both personal and

social lives.

However, it is also important to realise that as much as one can motivate himself, by both Intrinsic and extrinsic manner, there are some factors that tend to disturb his state of mind leading to growth of mob mentality or common frame of approach towards life rather than distinct approach.

The foremost factor is the thought of being a rebel or being isolated (due to individuality) From society. The thought of getting cornered because of different frame of thought processes is common.However, it is absolutely healthy to have a viewpoint that may be completely different. Also there is a constant feeling of being abnormal thinker. But in reality, it is this abnormal or different thought process that makes you distinct from others. As much as we say individuality is the best gift that one can give to his own self. It is an identity of a soul whose presence is felt only in its absence.

Delimit your boundaries and feel an essence. The feeling of being emotionally and decisively strengthened is what that a unique personality possesses.

IX

Adapting to a change

Nothing in this world or universe can ever remain constant. Nothing is permanent. Every single thing has to change one day or the other. It is meant to go that way only.Let us think of the water. If it remains stagnant at a particular place,

It becomes the breeding ground for a lot of diseases. But if it flows regularly, that is, changes its state of rest then it cannot compile any of the disease. Similarly if a change does not occur in your Life or surroundings then it maybe a sign of something wrong. Change is the law of nature.

Every particular thing, Be it place, feelings, achievement, position comes along with a limit of time. That is everything lasts for a specific period of time.

It is an old age saying that

"thistooshallpass".

Jazmin

This has a Context dealing with positive and negative aspects of life. When in grief, one must remember this quote and remind himself that this period of sadness, loss, grief or failure is just meant to happen and this moment will too pass away just like the other moments.

This realization is essential to be kept in mind because this quote can set up a frame of mind that will not fall into ever deepening path of negative and melancholistic thoughts and will help one to survive, with hope -the difficult times.

Not only in grief, but this is also helpful when one is in success phase of life. During such phase, a human being often tends to forget his roots And starts climbing up to the stairs of overconfidence which eventually leads to the tower of arrogance and evilness. However, a person must realise that without continuous efforts and hard work, no one can ever remain still on the peak of the success. However as it is said, the good times too can pass away but on the passing away of the good times, one must realise that it was meant to go. However, it is now essential to realise that one should not again fall into the face of sadness rather one should figure out ways to bring the good times again.

This all we discussed so far emphasises on the importance of change in one's life. If a change does not occur than a new phase won't enter into life of an individual. New phase brings along a lot new experience with it,. Emotions too grow throughout these new phases. Thus, change in life is crucial for inculcating new experiences, growing through the change emotionally and building a personality to a greater extent for practical life.

However, the effect or influence during The phase of change occurs on frame of mind

majorly. The thing to be kept in mind while during this phase of life is that everything happens for the good. With this thought in mind, one can easily go through such face without falling into a deep pit of negativity.

However, you might feel that something wrong is going around you. There will be times when you will question your self- esteem. there will be times when you will question yourself. This will be the time when you have to really control your Thought process. Your mind will think that you are not worth it. You will feel lost. You will think negatively. This will be the time, you

will feel the weakest. But don't let this affect you. If you were not worth the suffering. You feel. Then it would not have come to you. The sheer feeling of being upset about little things will upset you more. It's natural. Don't just think it abnormally. Don't take it negatively. The moment you gather courage to fight the brawl in your mind will be the moment that will lead you to the first step on the journey of the hustles that ultimately reaches the destination that is your dream or aim.The progressive journey in this path towards your aim ,is what is meant by success.

Now, question arises that how can one really not let the change affect him or her?The change or transition phase definitely brings behavioural changes in a person. But rather than this, the major impact occurs on one's point of view. The way how a person will deal with the situation and problems ahead in his or her life is set up during this phase only.

The sudden change will definitely Affect you. It will affect your mindset., your views, your perspective as already said. When a person is in the race for some competition, he or she cannot win it just by running on the day of such competition. It requires a huge number of effort that will progressively increase one's strengths, only if the effort made are in a positive way. This also doesn't mean that any effort submitted in this progress will ever go waste. The sum total of all the efforts you put through with a positive mindset and faithful intention will definitely make you shine on the day of race.

During the times when one is preparing for something great, as an example above, there will be few changes that were required to be incorporated in you.These changes can be

imposed upon your lifestyle or even the way you think.

But are there any options Other than adapting to the required change? Some may say that not necessarily, because it is all the luck that matters. But this is hardly hundred percent true to what I feel. In my opinion, being lucky about things getting happened to you Easily will not give you the happiness that the things you achieve with your hard work gives. The changes, after all to get successful , are must to have and adapt in life.

Let us think of an example of a farmer with a couple of hectares of fertile land and all the luxuries and facilities required for sowing, growing and harvesting the commercial crops. But for all the phases to go through, he has to make efforts right from sowing of the seed to harvesting it. All that would require humongous amount of hard work and labour. But if he denies all the efforts to be made and just relaxes by dreaming about the results by not putting any efforts, he would definitely be at loss. The effort has to be made so as to obtain the required results. For this, he has to take care of the field and put all his efforts to make his dream a reality.It was just A simple yet thoughtful example. One can now think in his or her mind the differences between dreaming and working

for making the dreams turn into reality. For these results that you want to get from the efforts you make, you might have to face a lot. Right from sacrificing comforts for putting a little more effort in your strategy to facing countless sleepless nights. The nights that kept you awakened would be the nights that would make you. For all these effort you might end up disturbing your sleep wake cycle and might even change your mindset too. But then you realise that this is the time which you can utilise, all these discomforts will gradually become a part of your life that will help you sleep comfortable nights. But how to adapt to these changes is very difficult question to be self answered.

But every question has its own answer.The things you can do to adapt to such changes are very simple yet perplexed. The major contribution made in disturbing you in such a phase is your own mind. The mind not only awakens the negative thoughts in you but also creates a barrier between your efforts and your goals. The persistent thoughts of negativity starts eroding the foundation of your effort. It affects your effort generating abilities to such an extent that you begin thinking about the negative consequences. The thing that might help you in stop doing so is the greatest power that a human could ever use. It is the power of putting these consequent negative thoughts to

their end. It is the power to calm your mind brain and heart. It is the power that everyone has, but only few realise it and only a minute fraction of people utilise it.

By This availability and utility of the power to calm human mind, we can easily classify human beings. There we go on to find three kinds of human that we find around us most of the times.

<u>Type I</u> – these are the people who don't really care about their strengths and only live in present, which is good sometimes. They don't realise or really care about future and importantly they Show human emotions like anger,Agony and negligence to a greater extreme.

<u>type II</u>-these are the people who know their potentials and powers. They do think of utilising their strengths for achieving the goals and dreams that they had set up. But conscious effort and the will to do so, is missing in them ,for most of the times. They just know how to do it why to do it and when to do it. But they just don't do it. If they do it ,they just reach a position where

they obtain a half of their desired results. Such people are often shy rather underconfident. Thus, this is the major reason of why they don't get their results satisfactorily.

Type III-these people, as already said, are present in only a few small fraction of population. Thus it can be appropriately said that these are the go- getter ones. They possess all the good qualities as type II persons have but apart from those qualities, they do possess some of the plus points that makes them different or special than others. These people do care about the consequences. These people also care about the importance of hard work to bring out the best . They reallywork hard for it. During the ups and downs of life, these people choose to stay strong by themselves. They choose positivity and stay away from even smallest of smallest negative thoughts.

People often get sad about the failures that come their way. Perhaps it is all normal to feel so. But, again, when you let these emotions of sadness overpower your journey, it becomes difficult for you to continue.

The main thing is to stay positive and think for the best and worst of the worst situations. The second important thing in adapting to the change is, enquiring or searching for the reason of this change. Just think about the fact that areThese changes in you meant for good? If you find a reason for your thought, you can easily find a reason to stay happy and not feel any burden during such times.Importantly, positivity is a choice. As told earlier, it is not the thing that is negative or positive, it is the way how you look at it and deal with it.

You cannot be morally and ethically correct every time. Being wrong is a human emotion as good as being right is. So, every day you Live, it is an opportunity. Learn to feel worth of every moment, you live. And be yourself and let all the positivity come into you. Exhale the negative thoughts. Adapt to a change that brings about the brawl in your Mind, with a positive mindset. Encourage yourself to push yourself a little more.

Never regret any kind of effort you put through. But apart from all these things,never hesitate to

talk. Never hesitate to share your state of mind to people who you trust. Talk about the issues you face To the right people, Sharing your experiences can help others to learn from you. So, every time you look back at your worst times, praise yourself with pride that you have successfully crossed that major hurdle.

X

Voids–the deflated places

If we go on to find the meaning of the word <u>void</u>, the dictionary would Probably tell us it as an empty space with nothingness residing in it. And that meaning is true in its own and many other context too.

Void is the definitely some empty space. To think it in a practical way,if we remove things from the space that it had occupied, empty space left behind Is what we say a void. Now thinking about it in an emotional aspect, one can definitely link it to departure of a closed one who leave their memories behind.

The sudden absence of such person or a thing or a pet or a habit or a routine or a comfort level makes a painful effect on the state of mind of a person going through it.Sometime we feel like this is all normal as it happens to every person when they go through such times. However, it is definitely not to be taken for granted.

Losing a person, particularly, who had once been so close to you, makes a voluminous impact in disturbing one's healthy mind. Since losing a person , In general, comes out as an utter shock and sometimes can result into fatalities as well, however there might be some other situations where you start realising that you have to Loseor erase or remove a memory that you may have become habitual of. Often this happens when one has to leave his or her habits of memorising some past moments.This too can put a burden on your thought process but usually it lasts Till you adapt a change. This occurs for a shorter duration of time and then a person should be back to normal routine but if that constantly bothers you especially when you are not doing that thing or are unable to reach out to your thinking, this leads to an unhealthy frameset of mind.

To begin talking on this topic,The major and dangerous impact that may lead a person to a deep bit of melancholistic thoughts, Should be discussed on priority. This is definitely on demise of an absolutely close person. Firstly, the acceptance part of this such phase is the most difficult as you might get so shocked in grief that you wander around as if nothing happened. This usually occurs when we find ourselves habitual of that person. All his things like habits, behaviour, aura, positivity, vibes attract you so strongly that you find yourself in an absolute state where you can't think of living without that person.

In such state, you become possessive about things and you start owing everything to that person. Absolutely ahead, you start finding ways out to express your affection in every possible way. Doing that iabsolutely normal and is a part of natural human emotions. But unfortunately if that person departs, it directly makes you think that there is no reason to live further. Because you had made somebody else the reason of your living existence, it bothers you so badly that you cannot make up a frame of mind that can accept the unfortunate loss. This can even shock or traumatise a person to a greater extent that could lead to fatality. But sooner or later, one has to accept the will of God. But even after this acceptance the consequent flashbacks of memories might haunt you.One may start

feeling emptiness residing in his or her body. A sense of nothingness worries him or her.

There occurs instances where you want to lead onto a normal life but the flashbacks hurt you. Then a feeling ofHopelessness develops In the mind. There is nothing that could bring him or her back. Such thoughts erode the foundation of one's individuality.

Moving in is easy than moving on

Jazmin

The destruction route is easy but the healing takes time.If you ever break a glass, it would split into pieces in no time but the same glass cannot be restored to its normal original condition. Similarly, a heart, a mind, a soul, can be disturbed by shocking incidents but unlike breaking of glass, our body can heal. But this process of growing through is slow. It needs continuous and worthy efforts in the form of intake of positivity. The series of flashbacks would definitely hurt but that does not affect you until and unless you let it bother you. Staying focused on the positivity of the life and the lessons that life teaches you, you can definitely rise above such loss.

Sometimes,A person, who is not so close to you and has nothing to do with your life, when dies, you start experiencing it as a personal loss. Many a times you start crying out for no reason and feel sad about his or her demise. This is because your mind was not prepared for it. However, nobody is prepared for anybody's death. But yet, the news might shock you. In such times, one needs to just meditate so as to detoxify his mind out of shock. One must realise that life is a precious gift which you get once. One life, one soul, one must make it immense in terms of every enjoyable aspect. Such incidents make us realise the worth of a life and the value of every person around us. This happens to make you realise the eminence of every tiny thing in your life.

Other aspects that can make you feel empty inside maybe the results of overthinking about certain things. Other than that, feeling of loss of interest usually arises. But how does overthinking creates Voids?

Well, there is an obvious answer to that. The fact that overthinking can disrupt you from the pathway of positivity, it is quite common that it may inculcate the never existing situations in your mind. This can be a reason why one cannot find any confidence in him. The thoughts like comparing to others in various terms like success, net worthOr even a good life can make you think that there is something missing out in your life. This creates a void. Such voids due to overthinking are generally not filled until one cuts down the reason of such thoughts. Overthinking is one such hazardous thing that can destroy a person from within. And to certainly get rid of such voids to accompany you, you must cut out the reasons for thinking in such a way.

Every time we think something, negative thoughts accompany our thinking and keeps us leading to a stage where we think us to be worthless. Such situations should be avoided. But this can only be done with the strengthened

frame of mind.

To build such a strong mindset is not an easy thing to do. It cannot be done as fast as one can say. After all Rome was not built in a day. Great things do take the time. They only occur to those who work hard for achieving such great things. However, it will reach you, only when it is destined to reach you. Staying strong by not disrupting positivity is must.

The voids left after some shocking incidents will definitely haunt you. But to get affected and imbalance your mind is only up to you.As said many a times earlier , that the intensity of a situation can be measured only after measuring the intensity of perception.

One must not feel shy to seek help. In tough times, only two entities can help you. The foremost being your own brain and mind and other being your close ones who really care about you.

However, a person goes on completing his journey on this road of life And Ultimately reaches death. This is a sad reality, A bitter truth.

One cannot replace a person but yes, the memories can be rejoiced by staying happy and saying good things and maintaining inner peace and positivity.

Life is a show, where you may come across many characters. But still remember, it is the show. Characters come and go. But the show must go on. Life never stops. You have to go along with it. Flowing rivers are always praised and adored.

The voids are definitely unfulfillable.The voids are unbearable. The voids are painful.But yet voids contain memories. It is not the nothingness that voids carry but an emotion to introspect and enjoy the flashbacks that follow.

XI

How does frame of mind helps?

Had you ever thought about how did you get that thought?

It may sound extremely rubbish but this is how a depth of any thought can be realised !!

Talking about the progenitor of all the things that you think upon, one can easily say that it is your mind that makes you think of anything. Well what exactly is this thing called mind?

Sometimes, this area, to define, is the most difficult task to do. However, one can say mind is the brains that a human has. Particularly, this is not true to a greater extent. But at least it is even for a lesser extent. Mind can be related to power that every human has.

> ***This is the power of consciousness, power of developing a sense for anything that may be visible or invisible,A power to think, power to express, power to perceive, Power to observe, a power to imagine, a power to generate andfeel emotions and importantly a power to keep a balance and act intelligently in stressful situations.***

Jazmin

Well, this is a simple definition to understand what exactly mind is. The importance to understand what mine does, is directly or indirectly related to the consequences of any situation.

But how does mind maintain psychological balance even in the situations of Sheer anxiety? Often we talk about the frame of mind or mind frame.

This is nothing but the orientation of the mind which defines or guides us to hypothetical path of rightness or wrongfullness.This orientation or adjustment of mind is done by the thought processes we generate within it.

Thus, it is usually seen that whenever a person is exposed to a situation, he thinks something or the other about it.We often see that person expresses his or her opinions or remarks either in the positive way or negative way spontaneously. this is because of the fact that the

mind of such person is oriented to take things either in a positive orbit or in a negative progression. But how is this orientation made? How is it not possible to remainpositive every time? How is it possible to not think negative.? Let's answer all these questions, in succession.

Firstly, this orientation of mind to think and perceive situations in any way is influenced by an avalanche of factors.The foremost factor comes right from the genes. Well, for the non science related individuals, genes are the transporter of parental information to the next generation. Genes are principally the most considerable factor that influence the mindset and thinking abilities.

In a research it was found that parents who had anxiety issues or melancholistic thought process, had children who grow up with negatively oriented thinking abilities.However this cannot be fully true as the genes can be influenced by a plenty of other factors as well. However, this is also not true that the parents who have a positive outlook into life will definitely Have the next generation same as them. The impact on the frame or orientation of

mind is greatly influenced by the environment during the growing phase of a child.The growing phase refers to the period of time when a child grows physically and mentally along with the development of mind. During this period a child is readily observant to all his surroundings and can build memories that remains in his subconscious throughout his lifetime. This can be understood from the fact that there are some instances which had happened tous in the childhood that we clearly remember. sometimes these instances can have an impact over the psychological abilities of a person. A traumatic incident faced in early childhood is like tearing a paper into pieces which then is glued together with time ,but the paper cannot remain as original it was.Similarly the instances that make a huge horrible impact on a child's mind cannot be forgotten throughout his or her life. The flashbacks that follow haunts him every time.

This canbe a reason of deferred mindset or anxious frame of mind even at a very young age. Another major impact on budding mind is the behaviour of parents.

During the younger phase of a person or even throughout his life,he learns a lot from his

parents or siblings. A child is seen copying his or her parents actions and readily adapts it to his or her own behaviour. This quality is helpful to teach the basic moral values and social etiquettes to a young one.

However,in the families where there are instances of conflict, contention and scrimmage, a growing child encounters a sense of maturity even before his or her teenage years. Such instances tend to disturb the peace of mind and start exaggerating a sense of brawl within the mind. A fear starts developing inside such human mind. This can be a reason of why a lot of youngsters throughout the world,are prone to anxiety issues and mental health anomalies.

Apart from this, in such years of growth, the school environment plays a crucial role too.

In many schools, especially in the indian schooling system, a person is trained to be a good crammer.Students are asked to ingurgitate and mug up all their syllabus and just write it all on

a piece of paper which will be a certificate of intelligence of a human. But that's just not the end, just students are harassed right from the nursery to the end of the professional studies for not being perfect and are even compared to the intelligent ones. *This continuous environment of harassing, scolding and brutally tearing off of Basic human dignity is just one side of the school or students life*.

Apart from this a major portion of the world is actively aware and worried about another evil called *bullying.*

Defining bullying is just necessary here because every single person has had experienced an incident of bullying. However they must have normalised it, For the sake of their own mental peace.

But bullying is just not the only reason of disturbing a human mind peace but also a weapon that murders the essence of individuality, humanity, dignity and importantly a social personality. This is however not right. This henios act is just not normal.

Rather it is just like an attempt of murder. It is just like firing a gun with silencer. The silencer might keep the noise silentBut the slaughter that it does is indescribable. The bulletshit the human emotions making them vulnerable to greater extent and slide them into an ever deepening grave.

He,whobullies,mustthinkbeforehedoes.The killing of a basic human emotion must be regarded as an ineffable and unforgettable infringement. This villiany act Might entertain the bullies for a short period of time but not to the people experiencing it. Instead of bullying others one must understand the dignity and pride of human soul. Bullies should know the worth of emotions of every single person on this earth.

Jazmin

A healthy interaction and a mutual respect can definitely help us to eradicate this evil. Nevertheless, One should always be hopeful and positive towards the journey of life.

Even if you had experienced bullying, you must not lose or defate the basic human spirit. You must not lose hope on humanity, neither should you let Your morals down. Never let anyone affect you so badly. Do not get hurt by anyone's judgement. They may pass their judgements on you but you have to make yourself aware that those who pass judgements are not go-getters like you. You are your own strength. Nobody can destroy your mind but your own thoughts can do so by constantly poking the negativity. So it is important to have control on thought process. This can be achieved by constantly reminding ones own mind to control and get away from negativity.

Never let your thought process be affected by others. Strengthen your mind to such an extent that nobody can influence you with their judgements. Learn to respect others opinions

but if it hurts you, never keep that In your head.

Let it be.

Other than these factors disturbing the basic orientation of human mind, the most important thing that is to be kept in vision,is the power that resides in the human soul. The power of feeling every emotion and having an opinion. The fact that every human mind is genius and has the potential to do wonders is just a few steps from realisation.Once you realise it, you can touch the heights of wonders and bring Ecstasy to your inner self and satisfy its desire of satisfaction.

The only requirement is framing of mind and bringing out the best in you.

Nevertheless, there is a scope of improvement every time. Surround yourself with memories, luxuries will follow you. Nothing is more greater than satisfaction which is the hardest yet simplest to achieve. The meaning of life is just not to do well in business or buy luxuries to surround you rather it is a journey of enjoyment

in whatever you have. Being rich and not satisfied is equal to running a race alone which has no finish line.

Satisfaction comes along a strong set of values, morals and importantly a stability of self consciousness.

9 798885 697941

Printed by Libri Plureos GmbH in Hamburg, Germany